# Destination Detectives

# Mexico

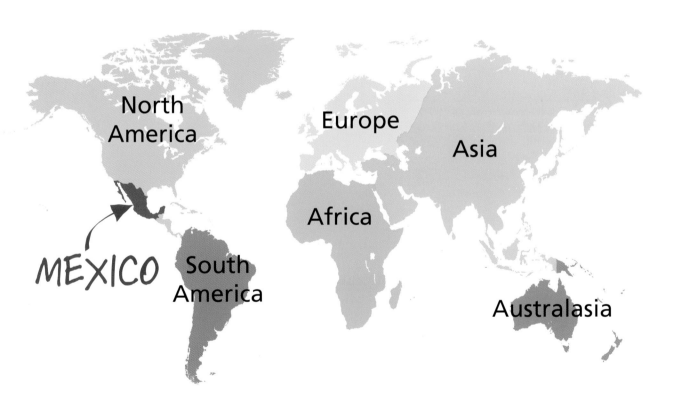

North America

Europe

Asia

Africa

MEXICO

South America

Australasia

Jen Green

**www.raintreepublishers.co.uk**
Visit our website to find out more information about **Raintree** books.

To order:
☎ Phone 44 (0) 1865 888112
📄 Send a fax to 44 (0) 1865 314091
💻 Visit the Raintree Bookshop at **www.raintreepublishers.co.uk** to browse our catalogue and order online.

First published in Great Britain by
Raintree, Halley Court, Jordan Hill,
Oxford OX2 8EJ, part of Harcourt Education.
Raintree is a registered trademark of Harcourt
Education Ltd.

Editorial: Melanie Copland and Lucy Beevor
Design: Victoria Bevan and Kamae Design
Picture Research: Hannah Taylor and Kay Altwegg
Production: Duncan Gilbert

Originated by Dot Gradations Ltd, UK
Printed and bound in China
by WKT Company Limited

ISBN 1 844 2141 17
10 09 08 07 06
10 9 8 7 6 5 4 3 2 1

**British Library Cataloguing in Publication Data**
Green, Jen
Mexico. – (Destination detectives)
972'.0841
A full catalogue record for this book is available from
the British Library.

**Acknowledgements**
ABPL p. 18 (Tony Robins); Action Plus pp. 26-27 (Neil Tingle);
Alamy Images pp. 20r (Brian Atkinson), 43 (britishcolumbia
photos.com), 20l (D. Hurst), 34 (Danita Delimont), 30-31
(John Arnold Images), 38-39 (PCL), 12-13 (Stock Connection);
Bridgeman Art Library pp. 10 (Father Hidalgo (mural), Orozco,
Jose Clemente (1883-1949) / Government Palace, Guadalajara,
Mexico, Mexicolore), 10-11 (Museo Nacional de Historia, Mexico
City, Mexico); Corbis pp. 8 (Bettmann), 38 (Bob Krist), 24
(Bohemian Nomad Picturemakers), 32-33 (Carl & Ann Purcell),
pp. 9l, 22-23, 41 (Charles & Josette Lenars), pp. 16-17, 18-19,
21, 33, 40, 42 (Danny Lehman), 29 (Gerald French), 35 (Gideon
Mendel), 5 (Gunter Marx Photography), 9r (Historical Picture
Archive), 13 (Kevin Schafer), 12, 27, 36 (Macduff Everton), 16
(Nik Wheeler), 15 (Owen Franken), 26 (Pablo San Juan), 28 (Phil
Schermeister), 31 (Randy Faris), 14-15 (Reuters), 36-37 (Robert
Holmes), 42-43 (Stephen Frink), 24-25 (Steve Starr), 7t (Tom
Bean); Corbis Royalty Free pp. 7b, 28-29; Harcourt Education Ltd
pp. 4-5, 6 (John Miller); www.visitmexicopress.com pp. 23, 30.

Cover photograph of cactus reproduced with permission
of Corbis/ B.S.P.I.

Every effort has been made to contact copyright
holders of any material reproduced in this book.
Any omissions will be rectified in subsequent
printings if notice is given to the publishers.

The paper used to print this book comes from
sustainable resources.

# Contents

Any words appearing in the text in bold, **like this,** are explained in the glossary. You can also look out for them in the Word Bank box at the bottom of each page.

# Welcome to Mexico

## Mariachi music

Mariachi music has been popular in Mexico for over a hundred years. The musicians play to crowds in town squares and cafes all over Mexico. Songs are played using guitars, trumpets, and violins. They often wear a traditional costume including a sombrero and a poncho (see photo on p. 5).

You wake up in a hotel room to the sound of music and singing. Looking out, you see a narrow street with brightly coloured buildings. A small band of musicians is strolling up the street!

## Where are you?

It is still early, with the morning sun striking the domes of a church in the distance. A man dressed in a poncho (huge shawl-type garment) is selling fruit on the street below. Further down, you can see a few shops with signs in Spanish.

A typical street in central Puebla, where your journey begins!

## Strolling players

The musicians are now passing. There are two men strumming guitars and one playing a violin. They are singing a sad song with Spanish words. Their clothes give you a clue – they are all wearing broad-brimmed sombrero hats, short jackets, narrow trousers, and cowboy boots.

This can only be Mexico! The musicians are one of the country's famous *mariachi* bands. When the song ends you ask them some questions. You find out that you are in the city of Puebla in the Central Highlands of Mexico. You have arrived just in time for a big fiesta (festival), for which the musicians are warming up.

### Ponchos and sombreros

Ponchos are traditional clothes worn by Mexican farm workers. A poncho is a square of woven cloth with a hole to put your head through. Sombreros are wide-brimmed hats that shield the head from the sun.

▲ Ponchos keep out rain and provide warmth in chilly weather.

# The land of Mexico

This is your first time in Mexico, and you do not know much about the country. The hotel has a tourist brochure, which includes a map of Mexico's different regions. You look at both over breakfast, when you have a *pan dulce*, a sweet roll.

## Size and shape

With a land area of nearly 2 million square kilometres (nearly 780,000 million square miles), Mexico is the world's fourteenth-largest country. It is shaped like a funnel – widest in the north, where it borders the United States. Guatemala and Belize lie on the southern boundary.

Mexico includes two large **peninsulas**. In the west, Baja California stretches far into the Pacific Ocean. In the east, the diamond-shaped Yucatan Peninsula juts into the Gulf of Mexico and the Caribbean Sea.

## Where do people live?

Mexico can be divided into three main regions:
- Much of the north is dry and **barren**, with few people.
- Most people live in the central area of the highlands. The capital, Mexico City, lies here, along with many other towns, including Puebla.
- The far south and the Yucatan Peninsula have fewer towns and villages.

**WORD BANK**    barren   bare land, with very little growing on it
colony   country that is controlled by another ruling country

Mexico is divided into 31 states and a federal district. Each state has its own government and its citizens elect their governor. The Federal District is a special political region where the capital, Mexico City is located.

Huge varieties of cacti are a common sight in the dry north of Mexico.

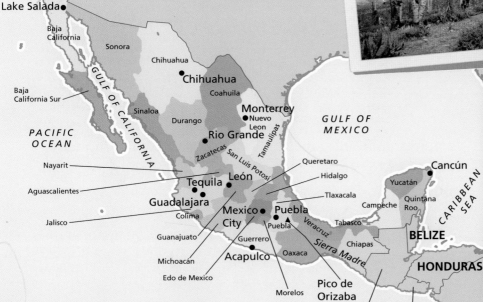

UNITED STATES OF AMERICA

Lake Salada

Baja California

Sonora

Chihuahua

Chihuahua

Coahuila

Baja California Sur

Sinaloa

Durango

Monterrey

Nuevo Leon

GULF OF MEXICO

PACIFIC OCEAN

Rio Grande

Tamaulipas

Zacatecas

San Luis Potosi

Nayarit

Queretaro

Hidalgo

Aguascalientes

Tequila

León

Tlaxacala

Cancún

Yucatán

Campeche

Quintana Roo

CARIBBEAN SEA

Guadalajara

Jalisco

Colima

Mexico City

Puebla

Puebla

Veracruz

Tabasco

BELIZE

Guanajuato

Guerrero

Michoacán

Acapulco

Edo de Mexico

Oaxaca

Sierra Madre

Chiapas

HONDURAS

Pico de Orizaba

Morelos

GUATEMALA

EL SALVADOR

N
W — E
S

0                    800 km

0                    500 miles

Cancun, on the Yucatan Peninsula, is Mexico's most famous beach resort.

## Mexico's population

Mexico's original **inhabitants** were Mexican Indians, who spread south from North America over 20,000 years ago. People arrived from Europe in the 1500s. For 300 years, Mexico was a Spanish **colony**. Now, most people are *mestizos* – people of mixed ancestry (see pie chart below).

Other (15%)

Mexican Indian (10%)

Mestizos (75%)

**inhabitant**  someone who lives in a place
**peninsula**  long, thin strip of land that sticks out to sea

# History

## Human sacrifice

People in ancient Mexico were very religious. The Aztecs worshipped their Sun god by performing human **sacrifice**. They cut out the hearts of their victims and offered them to the god.

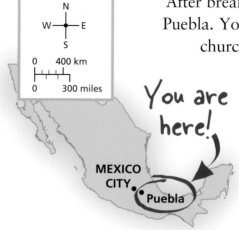

After breakfast you take a look around Puebla. You see a strange hill with a church on top. Someone tells you it is the Great Pyramid of Cholula – the remains of an ancient temple.

The tourist brochure tells you that Mexico was home to many great civilizations before 1600. They ruled mighty **empires** and built amazing cities that still stand in many parts of Mexico. First were the Olmecs, who carved giant stone heads. Later the Mayas built temples in the Yucatan. Last were the Aztecs, who ruled much of Mexico from the 1300s to the 1520s. They were conquered by Spanish soldiers called *conquistadors*.

## New Spain

The Spanish took over the Aztec empire and made it a Spanish **colony**. They captured more land to build a massive **territory** called New Spain. It included much of Central America, up to northern Panama, and much of the United States. All over Mexico the Spanish built European-style cities, with a square called the *zocalo* in the centre. You wander in to the centre of town to find Puebla's *zocalo*. You discover that the city was founded as Puebla in 1532.

The Aztecs believed that human sacrifice was necessary so that the Sun would rise every day.

**WORD BANK**    empire  group of countries ruled by a single country or ruler

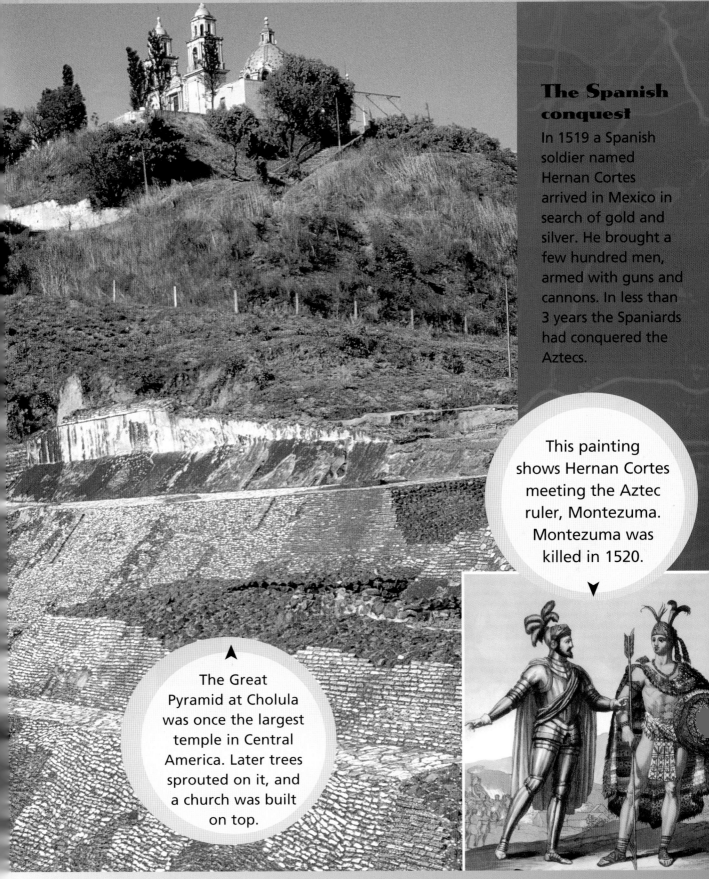

## The Spanish conquest

In 1519 a Spanish soldier named Hernan Cortes arrived in Mexico in search of gold and silver. He brought a few hundred men, armed with guns and cannons. In less than 3 years the Spaniards had conquered the Aztecs.

This painting shows Hernan Cortes meeting the Aztec ruler, Montezuma. Montezuma was killed in 1520.

The Great Pyramid at Cholula was once the largest temple in Central America. Later trees sprouted on it, and a church was built on top.

**sacrifice**  someone or something that is killed and offered to a god
**territory**  land that a country or ruler owns or controls

9

# Modern Mexico

In 1810 Father Miguel Hidalgo made a passionate speech from his church in Dolores in central Mexico, *"Mexicanos, viva Mexico!"* ("Mexicans, long live Mexico!") Every year Mexico's president repeats this rousing cry on Independence Day, which begins at 11 p.m. on 15 September, which celebrates freedom from Spanish rule.

In Puebla's main square you admire the Spanish cathedral. Continuing your stroll, you end up in the local Museum of the Revolution, which explains all about Mexico's more recent history.

## Spanish rule

Mexico remained a Spanish **colony** for 300 years. During this time life was hard for the Mexican people. They had to work on the land or in the mines that supplied Spain with silver and gold. In 1810 a priest named Miguel Hidalgo y Costilla called upon Mexicans to overthrow the Spanish. His speech started a rebellion. In 1821, after 11 years of fighting, Mexico won its **independence** from Spain.

Hidalgo's speech is known as the *grito de Dolores* – cry from Dolores.

**WORD BANK**   cavalry  soldiers on horses
**dictator**  ruler who has complete power over everyone and everything

# Early years of independence

The first century of independence did not bring peace for Mexican people. Mexico fought wars with the United Kingdom, France, Spain, and the United States, and lost over half of its **territory** to the United States. A **dictator** named Porfirio Diaz ruled Mexico for around 30 years from 1876. In 1910, Mexicans rose up against him. This was the Mexican Revolution. The fighting lasted until 1917, when the revolutionaries won.

## "Land and Liberty!"

Two soldiers led the Mexican Revolution. Francisco "Pancho" Villa was a brilliant **cavalry** officer. Emiliano Zapata encouraged Mexicans using the slogan *"Tierra y Libertad!"* ("Land and Liberty!")

In 1862 France invaded Mexico. Mexicans defeated the French at the Battle of Puebla. However, the French were victorious later the same year.

# Climate & geography

From high up you can see that Puebla is ringed by mountains. Is the rest of Mexico similar? You study a **relief map** on display in a local shop.

## Mountains and plateaus

Much of Mexico is mountainous, with over half the country above 1,000 metres (3,300 feet). There are two long chains of mountains, the western and eastern Sierra Madre. The Central **Plateau** in between covers a huge area, with cities such as Puebla found in **fertile** valleys. Even more mountain ranges lie in the far south and in Chiapas in the east.

### Underground Mexico

Mexico has lots of amazing cave systems, including many in the Yucatan Peninsula. Limestone-rich water dripping from cave roofs creates rocky stalactites hanging downwards (see below). Tall columns called stalagmites rise up from the floor.

### Fact box

*Highest mountain: Pico de Orizaba, 5,699 metres (18,696 feet) above sea level*
*Lowest point: Lake Salada, 10 metres (33 feet) below sea level*
*Coastline: 9,350 kilometres (5,830 miles)*

fertile  land that is good for growing crops on
plateau  area of high, flat land

# Rivers and lowlands

Mexico's longest river is the Rio Bravo (also called the Rio Grande). Flowing for 3,025 kilometres (1,880 miles), this river forms much of the border with the United States.

The Gulf Coast and Yucatan **Peninsula** are Mexico's biggest lowlands. In the Yucatan, water seeping through the **porous** limestone rock produces underground rivers. In some places, the roofs of these rivers have collapsed, creating rocky pools called *cenotes*.

## Copper Canyon

The *Barranca del Cobre* (Copper Canyon) is one of Mexico's most dramatic features. Located in the western Sierra Madre, it is made up of five linked canyons. Together they are five times wider, and one and a half times deeper, than the Grand Canyon in the United States.

*Cenotes* like this one have clear blue waters. These pools were holy places in ancient times.

The striking scene at sunset in the Copper Canyon.

**porous** rock that has tiny holes so that water can trickle through it
**relief map** map that shows where the land is higher or lower

## Birth of a volcano

Mexico's youngest volcano, *Paricutin*, is less than a century old. It began life as a smoking mound in a farmer's field in 1943. Since then it has grown to a towering mountain over 2,800 metres (9,200 feet) high.

The name *Popocatépetl* means "Old Smoky" in a local Indian language.

➤

# Volcanoes and earthquakes

Whoa! What was that? For a second the ground seemed to shake, but no one took much notice. Someone says it was a tremor – a small earthquake.

Out in the Pacific Ocean west of Mexico lies a deep **trench**. This trench is a boundary between two of the giant sections (called **tectonic plates**) that form Earth's outer layer. These plates meet and push together here. The enormous pressure causes earthquakes and volcanic **eruptions** in Mexico. Small tremors like the one you just felt are quite common. Major earthquakes hit from time to time.

**WORD BANK**  active  volcano that may erupt sometime in the future
dormant  volcano that is not expected to erupt again

# Smoking volcano

A line of volcanic mountains runs west to east across Mexico not far from Puebla. They include two tall, cone-shaped peaks that tower over the city. *Iztaccíhuatl* (known as Izta) is a **dormant** volcano. Neighbouring *Popocatépetl* (known as Popo) is **active**. You often see a plume of smoke rising from the mountain. In 1994 Popo showered Puebla with ash, and in 2000 villagers were evacuated because of an eruption.

Hundreds of buildings collapsed in the 1985 earthquake.

## Unlucky capital

In 1985, a major earthquake hit Mexico City, destroying the city hospital, government buildings, and thousands of homes. Over 6,000 people died and many more were injured.

Only about
10 centimetres
(4 inches) of rain a
year falls in northern
Mexico. Deserts stretch
for hundreds of
kilometres near the
US border. Parts of
southern Mexico
have the opposite
problem. Heavy
summer downpours in
Chiapas and Tabasco
can cause huge floods.

# Weather in Mexico

The midday sun is fierce in Puebla. Everyone wears hats and sunglasses. Many people take a Spanish-style *siesta* (snooze) after lunch. Things cool down late in the afternoon.

# Different climates

The main thing that affects the **climate** in different parts of Mexico is the height above sea level. The lowlands are the hottest areas, while high mountains are the coolest. Between the two, the Central Plateau has a mild climate, with warm summers and cool winters.

In parts of
south-east Mexico,
up to 400 centimetres
(157 inches) of rain falls
yearly. The high rainfall
allows lush forests
to grow.

climate  regular pattern of weather in a region
hurricane  fierce storm with very high winds

# Rainfall

Puebla gets quite a lot of rain, especially in summer. But many parts of Mexico have very low rainfall. This means that deserts and **scrubland** cover more than half of the country, mainly in the north.

# Spreading deserts

The deserts of northern Mexico are getting larger. Experts think this is linked to the world's climate getting warmer. Farms in the north also have to use a lot of water. This is reducing the amount of water found underground, which helps things to grow.

## Hurricane season

The Gulf and Pacific coasts of southern Mexico are sometimes hit by **hurricanes** in late summer. These tropical storms form out at sea, and then move inland causing great destruction. In 1995, coasts of the Yucatan were hit by two powerful hurricanes in the same year.

Mexico's highest mountain, Pico de Orizaba, shows the effect of height on climate. The top of the mountain is always covered in snow, while pine forests grow on lower slopes.

**scrubland** area covered in small trees and bushes

# Food & culture

It's now evening, and you're very hungry. Time to get to grips with Mexican cooking! Like much of Mexican culture, the local cooking is a mixture of Spanish and Indian. Tasty and often spicy, Mexican food is enjoyed around the world.

## Tortillas and beans

Mexico's main food is corn (maize), which is made into flat pancakes called tortillas. These are served in many different ways, filled or topped with cheese, meat, and spices. Beans and chilli are used in many dishes. Perhaps the most famous is chilli con carne (meat and beans in a hot chilli sauce).

## On the menu

• Tacos: tortillas rolled around fillings such as cheese, beans, vegetables, or meat with a chilli sauce

• Tostadas: flat tortillas toasted and piled with toppings such as cheese, beans, or spicy meat

• Guacamole: avocado dip

• Chiles rellenos: green chilli peppers stuffed with cheese or meat and spices, and then fried and served with a sauce

Lettuce, avocado, and sour cream garnish this taco.

➤

## Eating out

Mexicans love to eat out in restaurants. In cities the main meal is served in the evening. In the country, it is more often eaten at lunchtime. Food may be washed down with fruit juice, or adults may choose beer.

## Foods of Mexico

Europeans brought chickens, pigs, goats, wheat, garlic, and apples to Mexico. In return, Mexican foods such as chocolate, vanilla, and chilli peppers are now used in cooking worldwide. Tomatoes, avocados, beans, and peanuts also come from this part of the world.

### Mole sauce

*Mole* is a rich, dark sauce made of unsweetened chocolate, chilli, and over 30 herbs and spices. It is served with chicken and turkey. This sauce is said to have been invented right here in Puebla!

You can buy a huge variety of tasty snacks at almost any time of day in Mexico.

19

## China Poblana

Legend says China Poblana arrived in Puebla as a slave, having been captured by pirates. The outfit she was wearing – a frilly blouse and embroidered skirt – became the traditional dress of Mexican women. It's now mainly worn on fiesta days.

## Fiesta day

The next day is 5 May, or *Cinco de Mayo*. This is the anniversary of the day in 1862 when Mexican soldiers beat the French at the Battle of Puebla. Celebrations go on all over Mexico, but the biggest are right here in Puebla.

## Celebrations begin

The party begins early on fiesta day. A market springs up in the main square, selling handicrafts and special little snacks called *antojitos*. Wandering about town, you come across a church with a tomb inside. The tomb is supposed to be the grave of a 17th-century Asian princess called China Poblana. The national costume that many Mexican women still wear today was inspired by the way China Poblana dressed.

➤ Fireworks explode and firecrackers pop during the 5 May festival.

◄ Women show off their national costume during a parade at a fiesta.

## In full swing

A rodeo is held on the edge of town in honour of the fiesta. Meanwhile celebrations heat up in the main square. There's a parade with everyone in costume, including feathery Indian headdresses. People dance to the music of mariachi bands.

Best of all are the fireworks. In some Mexican cities these are wired on to tall frames shaped like castles. Here in Puebla they're attached to a bull costume worn by a man who charges the crowd. Firecrackers explode everywhere – exciting but very scary!

### Rodeos

*Charreadas* (rodeos) are held on fiesta days. Cowboys (*charros*), in splendid outfits, ride wild bulls or bucking bronco horses. Others show their skill with the lasso by roping bulls and other horses as they ride (see left).

## Important holidays and fiestas

**1 JANUARY:**
New Year's Day

**21 MARCH:**
Birthday of Benito Juarez, one of Mexico's early presidents

**MARCH/APRIL:**
Lent and Easter

**5 MAY:**
Battle of Puebla

**15–16 SEPTEMBER:**
Independence Day

**12 OCTOBER:**
Columbus Day

**1–2 NOVEMBER:**
Day of the Dead

**20 NOVEMBER:**
Revolution Day

**12 DECEMBER:**
Feast of Our Lady of Guadalupe

**25 DECEMBER:**
Christmas Day

# Religion and holidays

You go into a cafe to escape the fireworks! Several local people are there. You ask them about religion and festivals in Mexico.

## Catholic saints

Mexico has no official religion, but 90 percent of people are Roman Catholics. **Catholicism** arrived with the Spanish *conquistadors* in the 16th century. Mexico's best-loved saint is the Virgin of Guadalupe – the Virgin Mary, who is also Mexico's **patron saint**. A big *posada* (procession) is held in her honour in Mexico City on her fiesta day, 12 December.

These gruesome skulls are really quite sweet – they are made from chocolate and icing!

Catholicism the Roman Catholic religion, a form of Christianity

# Mexican festivals

Some fiestas celebrate great dates in Mexico's history, such as 5 May and **Independence** Day, which starts at 11 p.m. on 15 September and continues long into the next day. Most fiestas are Catholic saints' days. However, many Christian festivals also reflect traditional Indian beliefs.

Mexico's most famous fiesta, the Day of the Dead, is an example of this. On this day, Mexicans remember their dead relatives. Families prepare a feast and invite the spirits of the dead to attend. People light candles to guide the spirits home, and give sweets and chocolate in the shape of skulls.

## Bulls on the loose!

The town of Huamantla in south-east Mexico has a scary bull-running festival called *La Noche en que Nadie Duerme* – "the night when no one sleeps". On this night, bulls run loose through streets covered with flowers and coloured sawdust. When the bull heads towards you it's a mad scramble to get out of the way!

# Everyday life

The morning after the fiesta, it's back to normal life. The streets are crowded with adults and children heading to work or school. You stop to talk to some of them about jobs and schools in Mexico.

## Jobs and industry

In Puebla the biggest employer is a car factory. Mexico has many factories. They produce everything from vehicles to iron and steel, chemicals, clothing, and processed foods. Mexico City and large towns such as Monterrey are major industrial centres. So are the factories called *maquiladoras*, located near the US border. Here, US and Japanese companies employ Mexicans to make electronic equipment, clothes, and other products.

## Mining

Mexico is rich in **minerals** such as gold, silver, zinc, lead, and copper. There are large stocks of oil and natural gas both on land and offshore. Mining gives the country much of its wealth.

▲ Oil is mined offshore in the Gulf of Mexico.

# Schools

Education is free and **compulsory** for everyone between the ages of five and eleven. The Mexican government is keen for children to stay on at school for at least another three years on top of this. But after age eleven education is no longer free, and many poorer families cannot afford it.

Many children in the country are also too far away to attend school in the cities and towns. Instead, they can go to a *Telesecundaria*. Instead of being taught by a teacher, lessons are transmitted through a television in the classroom. In 1994, a powerful satellite was launched, which could reach even more remote villages. The new system had six channels, which were transmitted 24 hours a day.

## Rising numbers

In the late 1900s Mexico had one of the world's fastest-growing populations. Around 1910 the country had just 15 million people. By 1990 that figure had grown to a huge 80 million. Around 2000 it passed the 100 million mark. In the last few years the birth rate has started to slow down.

This *maquiladora*, in the Mexican border town of Tijuana, produces cars and trucks that are mainly sold into the United States.

**mineral** substance found in the ground, such as gold, silver, or zinc

# Time off & sport

## Jai alai

*Jai alai* is a fast, furious game a bit like squash. Players use curved rackets to strike the hard rubber ball. As in squash, the ball can be bounced off the walls of the court. The game originally came from the Basque region of Spain.

So what do Mexicans do in their free time, apart from celebrating fiestas? You come across a game of football being played in a quiet alley.

## Football crazy

*Futbol* (football) is Mexico's favourite sport. The game is played in every town and village, and there is huge support for league sides and the national team. Top matches take place in venues such as the Azteca Stadium in Mexico City. The "Mexican wave" was invented here during the World Cup in 1986.

*Jai alai* is a fast-paced game – the *pelota* (ball) can travel up to 290 kph (190 mph)!

## Other sports

Basketball, volleyball, and baseball are also very popular. Bull-fighting has been part of Mexican culture for over 500 years. Bull-fights, called *corrida de toros* by Mexicans, generally begin on December 25, and they continue every Sunday until April. To many, they are an exciting display of skill and bravery.

## Relaxing in Mexico

Some Mexicans keep fit by jogging. Whole families enjoy Spanish-style strolls, called *passeandos*, when temperatures cool in the evening. Towns such as Puebla have a lively nightlife with bars, cinemas, and nightclubs. Internet cafes are springing up even in sleepy towns.

## The Mayan ball game

The ancient Mayas had a ball game that was a cross between sport and a sacred ceremony. Two teams played with a rubber ball the size of a soccer ball. Players used hips and knees to bounce the ball though a hoop high on the wall. After the match, the losers, or sometimes the winners, were put to death in a religious **sacrifice**!

Mexican *futbol* fans enjoy the atmosphere at the 2002 World Cup in Japan.

The aim of the sacred Mayan ball game was to get the ball through a hoop like this one.

# Travel & cities

## Rural transport

You board a bus heading for Mexico City. The mix of vehicles on the road changes as you leave Puebla. Out in the countryside, donkeys, oxcarts, motorbikes, and bicycles are used to carry passengers and heavy loads.

You are now keen to see more of Mexico. The capital, Mexico City, is your first destination. You call in at the tourist office to find out about the best way to travel.

## On the road

The high mountain ranges make it difficult to build roads and railways that go across the country. Most major highways and rail routes run north to south, keeping to **plains** and valleys. The Pan-American highway runs the length of the country, linking Central America with the United States. Buses are one of the best ways of getting about, and also seeing the countryside. There are many different bus companies. In cities people often use shared taxis to get around.

Donkeys are used to help carry firewood in the countryside. ▼

**WORD BANK**    plain  large, flat area of land

# Rail and air

Mexico's rail network dates back to the late 1800s. Rail travel is cheap, but very unreliable. Only a few lines, such as the Copper Canyon railroad, run smoothly. Air travel is a great way of covering the huge distances inside Mexico for anyone who can afford the fares. Increasing numbers of people hop on a plane to travel between cities such as Mexico City, Monterrey, Merida, and Acapulco.

Colourful taxis are everywhere on this street in Mexico.

The Copper Canyon railroad runs for a total of 700 kilometres (435 miles).

## The Copper Canyon railroad

The rail route through the Copper Canyon has been called "the world's most scenic railroad". The 12-hour trip crosses 36 bridges and passes through 87 tunnels. On the way you see some of Mexico's most stunning scenery, including deep gorges and tumbling waterfalls.

## Sights of the capital

- Cathedral: the largest church in Mexico
- National Palace: Site of Mexico's government
- Templo Mayor: Remains of an Aztec temple
- Latin American Tower: 44 storeys high, the view from the top is fantastic
- Palace of Fine Arts (below): has some of Mexico's greatest art

N
W——E
S

0    400 km

0    300 miles

You are here!

MEXICO CITY

# Mexico City

Mexico City is one of the world's largest cities. The bus takes a long time to weave through the **suburbs**. Eventually you arrive in the centre of Mexico's capital.

# A historic city

Mexico City was founded by the Spanish in 1521. It is built on the ruins of the ancient Aztec capital, called Tenochtitlan, and on marshy land where a lake once stood. Mexico's capital has a mixture of Spanish **colonial**, 19th-century, and modern buildings. Buildings line the broad avenues that run through the city. As in other Mexican towns, the *zocalo* (main square) lies at the heart of the city.

# Ups and downs

There is a lot to see in Mexico City, but the capital also has its problems. Heavy traffic makes it difficult to drive in the centre. It's better to take the metro instead.

**Pollution** from cars and factories forms a blanket of smog (smoky fog) that hangs over the capital. Smog hides the surrounding mountains. On some days you can't even see the tops of tall buildings! Recently, laws have made it more difficult for people to use their cars in the city to ease traffic jams and lower pollution levels.

## That sinking feeling

Built on the soft, sandy bed of a drained lake, Mexico City is sinking. Just a century ago it stood 1 metre (3 feet) above the level of the lake. Now it is 3 metres (10 feet) below it. The city sinks about 15 centimetres (6 inches) every year.

▲ The ground around **Independence** Monument in Mexico City is sinking rapidly.

## Tequila

The town of Tequila, 50 kilometres (31 miles) west of Guadalajara, is where the alcoholic spirit of the same name was first made. Production of the drink started over 200 years ago. It is made from blue agave, a cactus plant with long bluish-green spiky leaves. Fields of this plant surround the town.

## Mexican cities

Besides the capital, Mexico has many other interesting cities that are worth a visit. You borrow a guide book to work out where to head to next.

## A typical Mexican city

Guadalajara to the west is Mexico's second-largest city. Located in a high valley, it has a mild **climate**. The city has a small centre with landmarks dating from the 1500s. Guadalajara is home to many typically Mexican things, including mariachi music, which can be heard all over town.

The pace of life is relaxed in Guadalajara. Old Spanish buildings edge the squares.

## Monterrey or Acapulco?

In the north-east, Monterrey is a busy city with spectacular rugged mountains surrounding it. There are huge squares with mainly modern architecture. A tall tower called the Beacon of Commerce shoots laser beams around the city at night.

In the south-west of Mexico, Acapulco is the country's most famous resort. It is known for its sandy beaches and lively nightlife. Although it is located on the Pacific coast, it is not that far from the capital. You decide to head for Acapulco. You pack your bags and hop on a bus.

Divers plunge a massive 40 metres (130 feet) off the cliff at La Quebrada.

### Divers of La Quebrada, Acapulco

Acapulco is famous for its daring divers, who plunge into the sea from a steep cliff called La Quebrada. Dives must be timed just right to catch the incoming waves, or the diver will land on the rocks underneath the surf!

## Jose Clemente Orozco

Mexican artists such as Jose Clemente Orozco (1883–1949) were inspired by great events in history, such as the Mexican Revolution. Orozco's most famous painting, shown on p. 10, shows Miguel Hidalgo, who called for revolt against the Spanish. The artist's work can be seen in Guadalajara, and also in the United States, where he lived for a time.

► This mural in the Presidential Palace is by Diego Rivera, one of Mexico's most famous artists.

0  400 km

0  300 miles

You are here!

MEXICO CITY•

•Acapulco

# City life

Even the lively, modern city of Acapulco has an old centre, dating back to the early days of Spanish rule. Spanish ships used the port in the 1500s, bringing silk and spices from China and the Philippines.

Acapulco's old town lies behind the harbour. There is an old fort and a main square with a few public buildings. Some of these buildings are decorated with murals (wall paintings), often by famous artists such as Jose Clemente Orozco.

**WORD BANK**  shantytown  area where the conditions are dirty and overcrowded, and houses are shacks

The number of people living in Mexican cities has grown rapidly in the last 50 years or so. In 1950 just 43 percent of Mexico's population lived in cities and towns. By 1975 that figure had soared to 63 percent. Over 75 percent of all Mexicans were living in cities and towns by 2000.

This woman's home in the slums overlooks the glamour of Acapulco beach.

## Expanding cities

Like many Mexican cities, Acapulco has grown a lot in recent years. Since the 1950s, huge numbers of Mexicans have moved to cities from **rural** areas, in search of work and a better life. However, many people end up without a job, living in the poor **shantytowns** (slums) that have grown up on the edges of cities. Homes in these slums, called "lost cities", have no electricity or running water. Even glitzy Acapulco has its share of slums.

# Rural life

You catch the bus back towards central Mexico. The road winds up the hills through farms and forests. Looking back, you can see fishing villages lining the blue coast.

## Fishing

Fishing has been a major industry since the 1960s. The waters around Baja California are rich in tuna, sardines, anchovies, and red snapper. Shellfish such as squid and lobster are also caught. Shrimping, too, is big business along the Gulf of Mexico.

## Harvesting chicle

Tree sap called chicle, which is often still used to make chewing gum, comes from *sapodilla* trees grown on **plantations** in Mexico. The milky sap oozes from cuts in the bark. It is collected in little cups and then processed to make chewing gum.

A worker cuts into a *sapodilla* tree to harvest chicle.

export when a country's products are sold abroad

# Farming

You pass through rugged mountains where small farms dot the hillsides. Two main types of farming go on in Mexico. Most farms are small plots where local people grow maize, beans, squash, and potatoes to feed their families. At the other end of the scale are the big estates, where cotton, wheat, coffee, and sugarcane are grown for **export**.

Small-scale farmers work the land using hoes and other simple tools, and ploughs pulled by horses. Large-scale farms can afford expensive machinery such as tractors and sprinkler systems to water the land.

# Forestry

Many of Mexico's forests are being cut down for wood. The pine forests of central Mexico provide cheap timber. Valuable woods, such as pine and oak, grow in the rainforests of the south-east.

## Ranching

Cattle are kept on huge ranches in parts of Mexico where the land is too poor to grow crops. In the north, beef cattle are reared for their meat, some of which goes to the United States. Dairy cattle are reared on cleared forest land in the south.

Fishermen haul in their recent catch at a fishing harbour in Baja California.

## Market day

You visit a local market, called a *tiangui*. People come from miles around to sell home-grown fruit and vegetables, hand-made pottery, and weaving. Also on show are cooking pots, cheap clothing, shoes, farm tools, and radios. You name it, you can buy it here!

# Country life

The beautiful scenery makes you decide to spend a few days in the countryside. The bus drops you in a tiny village. It is like entering another world!

Just about everything is different in the country. In cities, most Mexicans wear modern clothes. In the country, however, women wear long skirts, loose blouses, and *rebozos* (shawls). Men wear cotton shirts, trousers, sandals, and sombreros. Most village houses are simple buildings one or two storeys high. Some are made of adobe, which is a type of clay brick that is dried in the sun.

# Village life

Most country people are farmers. Families keep a few animals such as chickens or a pig, mostly for their own needs. Any spare eggs, fruit, or vegetables are sold at the local market. Family life is important. Grandparents often live with their grown-up children and help raise the grandchildren. Young people often live at home until they get married.

Women in the countryside carry their babies in slings made from woven *rebozos*.

## Land rights

Since the revolution most farmland in Mexico has been owned **communally**. The shared land is called *ejidos*. Each farmer has rights over a small plot, which later passes to the farmer's children. Changes introduced in the 1990s meant that some farmers now own their land.

# Tourism & travel

At the local market you link up with a few other tourists. You go to a cafe to swap ideas about all the great places still left to visit in Mexico.

## Mayan ruins

The Yucatan has hundreds of Mayan sites, only some of which have been uncovered. Others still lie deep in the jungle! Palenque and Chichen Itza are the most visited. *La Ruta Maya* is a tourist trail linking the best sites.

## Spectacular ruins

Top of the list for many tourists is a visit to one of Mexico's ancient cities. You can see Olmec ruins at La Venta in the south. The amazing city of Monte Alban in Oaxaca was built by the Zapotecs. The Mayas built many temples all over the Yucatan. Experts are unsure who built the spectacular pyramids of Teotihuacan, 50 kilometres (33 miles) from Mexico City.

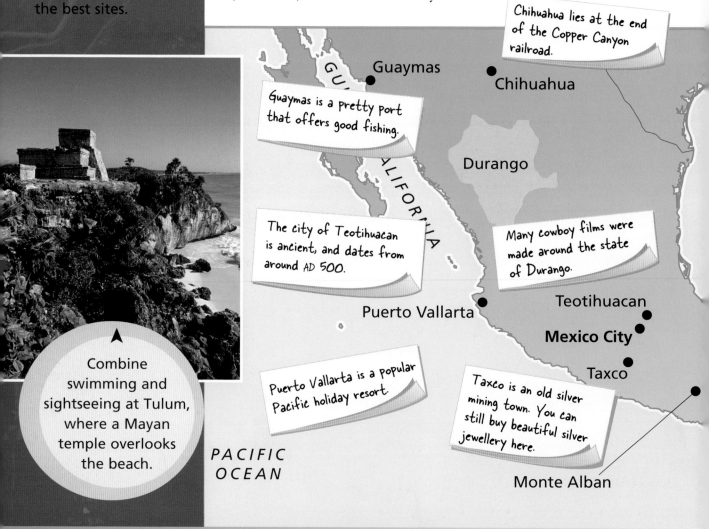

Combine swimming and sightseeing at Tulum, where a Mayan temple overlooks the beach.

Chihuahua lies at the end of the Copper Canyon railroad.

Guaymas

Chihuahua

Guaymas is a pretty port that offers good fishing.

Durango

The city of Teotihuacan is ancient, and dates from around AD 500.

Many cowboy films were made around the state of Durango.

Puerto Vallarta

Teotihuacan

Mexico City

Taxco

Puerto Vallarta is a popular Pacific holiday resort.

Taxco is an old silver mining town. You can still buy beautiful silver jewellery here.

Monte Alban

PACIFIC OCEAN

# New horizons

Mexico is a huge country with very varied landscapes. You have seen parts of the Central Plateau, but the scenery elsewhere is also breathtaking. There are the cactus-dotted deserts of the north; the craggy mountains of the Sierra Madre; the lush rainforests of the south-east; and the blue, rocky *cenotes* of the Yucatan.

## Flying men of Papantla

At Papantla in east-central Mexico you can see the amazing dance of the *voladores*, or "flying men." Four men wearing bird costumes launch themselves from a high pole with ropes around their waists, and circle downwards. It is seriously scary!

N
W — E
S

0                    800 km
0                    500 miles

UNITED STATES
OF AMERICA

GULF OF
MEXICO

Mérida is a good place for exploring Mayan ruins.

Cancún is the biggest holiday resort in the Yucatan.

Cancún

La Venta   Mérida

CARIBBEAN
SEA

Palenque

BELIZE

HONDURAS

EL SALVADOR

GUATEMALA

41

# Stay, or go home?

You've seen a bit of Mexico, including Puebla, Acapulco, and the capital. But Mexico is a big place, and there is still a lot more to see and do! It's decision time: do you hop on a plane for home, or sample more of Mexico?

## Great days out

You make a shortlist of must-do activities. It includes snorkelling at the coral reefs of the Yucatan, where you can also explore underground caves. On both the Pacific and Gulf coasts you can hire a boat to fish for tuna and marlin. Or you can paddle a kayak between the islands off the coast of Baja California. Take a hike in the Copper Canyon, or scale the great peak of Orizaba – the choice is yours!

## Highlights of the National Parks (NP)

**Agua Azul NP:** jungle waterfalls

**Sian Ka'an Reserve:** tropical forests and mangrove swamps

**Cascada de Basaseachic NP:** Mexico's second-highest waterfall

**Copper Canyon NP:** fantastic canyon scenery

**El Rosario, Michoacan:** monarch butterfly sanctuary.

◄ Thousands of monarch butterflies cling to a tree in the Michoacan sanctuary.

**WORD BANK**    lagoon *pool of water by the sea*

# Wildlife-watching

You haven't yet seen much of Mexico's wildlife. At El Rosario in Michoacan you can see monarch butterflies that have flown all the way from Canada. Scammon's **Lagoon** in Baja California is the place for whale-watching. Grey whales give birth to their calves here in winter. You can also catch a glimpse of monkeys and parrots in the rainforests. Flamingos and pelicans make their nests along the coast.

◄ A grey whale and her calf enjoy the warm waters of Scammon's Lagoon.

## Holiday ideas

- Go white-water rafting in Veracruz, to the ruins of El Cuajilote, best seen from the river.
- Scuba-dive off Cozumel Island in the Yucatan – one of the world's largest living coral reefs.
- Or, you can dive to explore the underground caves of the Yucatan.
- Try rock climbing on sheer rock walls near Tijuana or Monterrey.
- Hike up the volcanic peak of *Iztaccihuatl*

**mangrove swamp** swampy area found along tropical seacoasts with a huge variety of trees, shrubs, and wildlife

# Find out more

Eager Destination Detectives can find out more about Mexico by using the books, websites, and addresses listed below:

## World Wide Web

If you want to find out more about Mexico, you can search the Internet using keywords such as these:

- Mexico
- Yucatan Peninsula
- Mexico City

You can also find your own keywords by using headings or words from this book. Try using a search directory such as **yahooligans.com**.

## Films

*Like Water for Chocolate* (1992)
An epic story of love and loyalty during revolutionary times in northern Mexico

*Night of the Iguana* (1964)
A haunting adventure set in Mexico. This American director's long fascination with Mexico began with the classic film *Treasure of the Sierra Madre* (1948).

## The Mexican Embassy

The Mexican Embassy in your own country has lots of information about Mexico, for example about the different regions, the best times to visit, special events, and Mexican culture. Embassies in many countries have their own website.

The UK embassy website is:

**www.mexico.embassyhomepage.com**

## Further reading

The following books are packed with information about Mexico:

*Country Insights: Mexico*, Edward Parker (Wayland, 1997)

*Discovering: Mexico*, Marion Morrison (Zoe Books, 1996)

*Explorer: Mexico*, Fiona Dunlop (AA Publishing, updated regularly)

*Nations of the World: Mexico*, Jen Green (Raintree, 2003)

*The Changing Face of: Mexico*, Edward Parker (Hodder/Wayland, 2001)

# Timeline

**around AD 300–900**
Mayan culture flourishes in southeastern Mexico.

**1340s**
Aztecs found the city of Tenochtitlan (now Mexico City) and rule a large **empire** from this capital.

**1519**
An army of Spanish *conquistadors* (soldiers) led by Hernan Cortes lands on the Gulf coast and heads towards the Aztec capital.

**1521**
Spanish *conquistadors* conquer Tenochtitlan. The Aztec empire becomes the core of the Spanish colony of New Spain. Spain rules Mexico for nearly 300 years.

**1540s**
The Spanish discover gold in New Spain. Huge amounts of gold and silver are shipped over to Spain.

**1810**
Miguel Hidalgo y Costilla begins Mexico's struggle for independence with his speech, the *grito de Dolores* ("cry from Dolores").

**1867–1872**
Maximilian is overthrown and Benito Juarez becomes president again.

**1862**
France invades Mexico. Mexican troops defeat France at the Battle of Puebla, but the French win later the same year. They make an Austrian archduke, Maximilian, emperor. He rules for three years.

**1855–1864**
A lawyer called Benito Juarez, from the Zapotec Indian tribe, is president of Mexico.

**1846–1848**
The United States wins a war against Mexico and takes much of Mexico's territory.

**1836**
The Mexican **territory** of Texas wins independence and becomes part of the United States.

**1821**
Mexico wins **independence** after 11 years of fighting.

**1876–1911**
The **dictator** Porfirio Diaz now rules Mexico.

**1910–1917**
The Mexican Revolution takes place. The revolutionaries overthrow Porfirio Diaz.

**1917**
Mexico adopts its constitution.

**1929**
The National Revolutionary Party (PRM) is formed and wins control of Mexico. In 1946 it becomes the Institutional Revolutionary Party (PRI). It remains in power until the year 2000.

**1934–1940**
President Lazaro Cardenas of the PRM introduces many new changes, including giving back land once owned by farmers.

**1958**
Mexican women get the vote for the first time.

**2000**
The PRI loses the elections. President Vicente Fox of the National Action Party is elected. Mexico makes a new free trade agreement with the European Union.

**1994**
Indian revolutionaries from the state of Chiapas revolt, demanding better living conditions.

**1993**
Mexico and the United States make an important trade agreement, called the North American Free Trade Agreement (NAFTA).

**1988**
**Hurricane** Gilbert strikes the Yucatan **Peninsula**, killing about 200 people.

**1985**
A major earthquake hits Mexico City, killing 6,000 people.

**1968**
Mexico hosts the Olympic Games.

# Mexico – facts & figures

Mexico's flag has been used since 1821, when Mexico became independent from Spain. It has three vertical stripes: green for independence; white for religion; and red for union (left to right). The coat of arms in the centre represents a legend – the Aztecs built their capital Tenochtitlan (now Mexico City) where they saw an eagle sitting on a cactus eating a snake.

## People and places

- Population: 104.9 million.
- Mexico City is the oldest capital city in the Americas, and the largest capital city in the world.
- Average life expectancy: 74.9 years

## What's in a name?

- Mexico's original name was Meshtleeko. However, the Spanish conquistadors could not pronounce this, and so changed the name to Mexico! The official name of Mexico is Estados Unidos Mexicanos, or the United Mexican States.

## Money matters

- Average earnings:
  Men – £7,473 (US$13,152)
  Women – £2,828 (US$4,978)

## Food and health

- Mexico introduced chocolate to the world.
- The Spanish brought the smallpox illness to Mexico, which killed many of the Indians.
- The average Mexican drinks more bottles of Coca Cola in a day than any other nationality in the world!

# Glossary

**active** volcano that may erupt sometime in the future

**barren** bare land, with very little growing on it

**Catholocism** the Roman Catholic religion, a form of Christianity

**cavalry** soldiers on horses

**climate** regular pattern of weather in a region

**colony** country that is controlled by another ruling country

**communally** owned by all the people who work on it

**compulsory** something you have to do

**dictator** ruler who has complete power over everyone and everything

**dormant** volcano that is not expected to erupt again

**empire** group of countries ruled by a single country or ruler

**export** when a country's products are sold abroad

**fertile** land that is good for growing crops on

**gorge** deep, narrow valley between hills or mountains

**hurricane** fierce storm with very high winds

**independence** country free from control of another country

**inhabitant** someone who lives in a place

**lagoon** pool of water by the sea

**mangrove swamp** swampy area found along tropical seacoasts with a huge variety of trees, shrubs, and wildlife

**mineral** substance found in the ground, such as gold, silver, and zinc

**patron saint** saint who is believed to protect a place, job, or activity

**peninsula** long, thin strip of land sticking out to sea

**plain** large, flat area of land

**plantation** area where crops such as tea, rubber, or *sapodilla* trees are grown

**plateau** area of high, flat land

**pollution** release of harmful chemicals into the air, ground, or water

**porous** rock that has tiny holes so that water can trickle through it

**relief map** map that shows where the land is higher or lower

**rural** to do with the countryside

**sacrifice** someone or something that is killed and offered to a god

**scrubland** area covered in small trees and bushes

**shantytown** area where the conditions are dirty and overcrowded, and houses are shacks

**suburb** built-up area on the edge of a town or city

**tectonic plate** one of the huge slabs of rock that make up Earth's outer layer, which is called the crust

**territory** land that a country or ruler owns or controls

**trench** deep furrow or ditch in the ground

# Index

# Titles in the *Destination Detectives* series include:

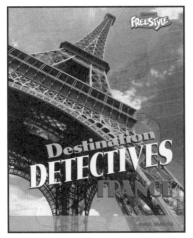

Hardback      1 844 21407 9

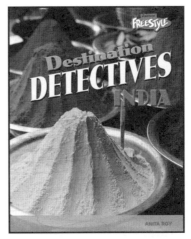

Hardback      1 844 21406 0

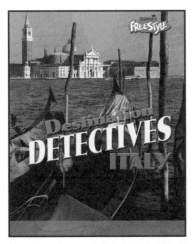

Hardback      1 844 21409 5

Hardback      1 844 21410 9

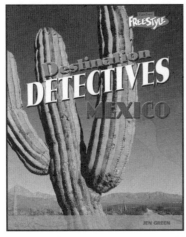

Hardback      1 844 21411 7

Hardback      1 844 21408 7

Find out about the other titles in this series on our website www.raintreepublishers.co.uk